KJV Translators to the Reader

© Copyright 2020 ● Dr. Jim Taylor

All Scripture quotes are from the King James Bible except those verses compared and then the source is identified.

Although a number of other authors have been quoted or mentioned in this book, this author does not share or endorse the various theological positions of everyone who is mentioned. Additionally, it can be reasonably assumed that those mentioned would not necessarily agree with every position or viewpoint mentioned herein. The mere citing or mention of others is NOT to be considered an endorsement of their beliefs.

The KJV Translators to the Reader

A Translator's Commentary

- *The spelling and the use of italics have been modernized in many cases (but not all).*

- *The subject headings (which were originally set in the margins) are placed in the body of the text.*

- *The scripture references in the margin are inserted in the text in square brackets.*

- *The many references to works of the early church writers which appeared in the margins have also been inserted with brackets.*

Footnote Commentary by Dr. Jim Taylor

Introductory Explanation   4

The Best Things Have Been Calumniated   9

The Highest Personages have been Calumniated   14

His Majesty's Constancy, Notwithstanding Calumniation, for the Survey
of the English Translations   16

The Praise of the Holy Scriptures   18

Translation Necessary   23

The Translation of the Old Testament out of the Hebrew into Greek   24

Translation out of Hebrew and Greek into Latin   29

The Translating of the Scripture into the Vulgar Tongues   31

The Unwillingness of Our Chief Adversaries, that the Scriptures Should
Be Divulged in the Mother Tongue, etc.   35

The Speeches and Reasons, both of Our Brethren, and of Our Adversaries against this Work   36

A Satisfaction to Our Brethren   39

An Answer to the Imputations of Our Adversaries   43

The Purpose of the Translators, with their Number, Furniture, Care, etc.
53

Reasons Moving Us To Set Diversity of Senses in the Margin, where
there is Great Probability for Each   57

Reasons Inducing Us Not To Stand Curiously upon an Identity of Phrasing   61

Commentator's Epilogue   66

Introductory Explanation

You may wonder why anyone, myself included, would want to take a letter which is so readily available in many different forms, and then add comments to what is written therein, and then go through the trouble of having it published. Especially since this letter from the King James translators to the reader is so readily available for free on the internet.

But the answer is simply this. I am a Bible translator. I have been involved in the actually translation work in several translations in the languages of Korean Chinese, Telegu, and Ewe. It has always been my desire to see whatever translation work I am assisting with be as good as the King James Version. In my mind, it is the gold standard of what a translation should be.

So naturally, I wanted to know as much about the processes and philosophy of the KJV translation team as possible. In the process of research, I found that two sources were very helpful. The first is a letter written by the translators to the reader (the basis for this small book). The other is a book called "Translating for King James" which is basically a compilation of John Bois' notes.

Whereas Bois' notes required a lot more time and meditation to grasp the reasons behind the translators' various word choices, the letter is fairly straightforward. And I suppose this is the main reason for its prominence in print.

In all of my years of study in the areas of textual analysis and Bible translational processes, I have seen this very same letter used by a number of so-called scholars to "prove" their own preferred viewpoints.

And I suppose that seeing there were at least 47 translators (it is believed that 54 were invited to help in the project, but in the end, only 47 actually did the work) who were broken into six teams, it is entirely possible that a variety of opinions could have been included in their letter to the readers.

But in the end, before this letter was included into the printed editions of the King James Version, these men would have had to come to an agreement as to where they, as a team of translators, drew their line in the sand.

It is a bit sad that the majority of the printed editions of the King James Version does not contain this phenomenal letter from the translators to the readers. It is filled with so much useful information on what they did and why they did it. It helps to explain their philosophy toward translation work and the translation itself.

So, this letter stands as the representative position of their collaborative work. This is the official viewpoint of the official team that translated the Authorized King James Version.

Thus, this document provides for us a wonderful explanation of a great many areas that a translator must consider when doing such a monumental work. Frankly, I doubt that many would fully agree with their point of view today. But their point of view resulted in the greatest translation of all time. And regardless of how one may feel about the Bible translation issue, there has never been another English translation that has made more of an impact on society, culture, or religion. The Authorized Version is the king of translations.

The translators of the King James Version made statements concerning their use and acceptance of previous translations. They spoke of the amount of emphasis that should be placed on the original languages. They commented on whether or not former works or commentaries ought to be used, and so on. And as a Bible translation consultant, I can tell you firsthand, that these are areas that translators still deal with today.

Consequently, this information is quite helpful for modern translators. Many modern translators look to the guidance and wisdom of these translators as they approach the task of translation themselves. It is not that these men were perfect but their translational work is exceptional, above reproach.

I have in my possession a book containing the notes of one of the King James translators. The title page points out that it is a true copy of the only notes made by a translator. This particular translator was John Bois. He could read the Bible in Hebrew by the age of five and was so gifted in Greek that he could turn to any Greek word in the New Testament at will.

Of all the translators involved with the KJV, as far as we know, he was the only person to have left for us a copy of his notes. He made these notes during the final review of the books of Romans through 2 Peter.

Between John Bois' notes and this letter from the KJV translators to the reader, we can get a pretty good idea of the general philosophy that the team espoused. And I have to say, from a modern translator's perspective, it is quite helpful and enlightening.

Again, it is not that these men knew everything there is to know but none would be able to successfully accuse them of ignorance either. These men are considered to have been some of the most educated and intelligent men of their day. This is especially true in the area of languages.

In the course of my own personal studies, I have seen this letter used by both friend and foe of the Authorized Version in order to support their own particular point of view. But I believe this letter should be considered in the historical context of which it was written.

These men did not argue over Greek manuscripts because at the time, the only Greek text in use was what we call the Textus Receptus. I realize that the translators actually used Theodore Beza's updated version of Erasmus' Greek manuscript but for all intents and purposes, it was basically the Textus Receptus minus a number of revisions which would come later.

They did not quibble over the theories of Dynamic Equivalency or Formal Equivalency either because in their day, it was understood that the most formal, word-for-word translation should always be done, whether it was the Word of God or any other document.

This is not to say we cannot find examples of dynamic equivalency in the King James Bible, for there most certainly are. But by and large, the translation itself is a great literary work of formal equivalent philosophy coupled with beautiful expressions of readability.

I believe that inasmuch as possible, we should allow these men to speak for themselves. There is much upon which we would agree. There are a few things upon which would probably disagree. These men were men. Fundamentally, they were no different from us - imperfect saints seeking to do their best for the Lord.

But, in bringing these men together to do this work, it is said that no team of scholars has ever reached their level of skill or understanding in the area of languages. Whereas those who seek to find fault with the King James Version today couldn't hold a candle to *one* of these men and certainly not to their translation team as a whole.

In summary, I believe that this letter could be of great value to anyone who is interested in knowing what kind of processes went into the translational work of the King James Version. I also believe it would be an invaluable piece of advice for any translator, or team of translators, who desire to produce in another language, a Bible that is of the same quality as the King James Version.

Modern translators should be able to look to the example of these men, not only in their approach to translation, but also in their humility. For you cannot read through this letter to the readers without coming away with a sense of their humility as they approach the work.

The Best Things Have Been Calumniated[1]

Zeal to promote the common good, whether it be by devising anything ourselves, or revising that which hath been laboured by others, deserveth certainly much respect and esteem,[2] but yet findeth but cold entertainment in the world. It is welcomed with suspicion instead of love, and with emulation instead of thanks: and if there be any hole left for cavil to enter, (and cavil, if it do not find a hole, will make one) it is sure to be misconstrued, and in danger to be condemned.[3]

---

[1] It is a fairly well-known fact that the translators were a mix of Anglicans and Puritans. Their theological viewpoints would most likely therefore have been a mixture of Calvinism and Arminianism. But all of these men were highly educated in languages and theological beliefs. But the personal beliefs of the translators had nothing to do with the accuracy of their translational work or the quality of the underlying text. I do not believe it is possible to demonstrate that their personal bias influenced their work in any way. In fact, it would be easier to prove the opposite.

[2] I am certainly no fan of modern translations yet I would hope we could at least begin with an understanding that at least some of the modern translations are **not** the result of evil men or money-making schemes. There truly are good men on both sides of the translation issue and though we would disagree with their position or method of ministry, we can at least allow them the benefit of standing in their integrity.

[3] The KJV translators fully understood that no matter how noble their motives in trying to be a help to others, they would actually be reviled. This is a lesson to anyone who would seek to translate the Scriptures into another language. You will be hated by many and loved by only a few. The work of spreading God's Word has never gone unchallenged. If the devil cannot use his people to bring the work to a halt, he will seek to cause turmoil among God's people. Every translator needs to be on guard against the wiles of the devil.

This will easily be granted by as many as know story,[4] or have any experience. For, was there ever any thing projected, that savored any way of newness or renewing, but the same endured many a storm of gainsaying, or opposition? A man would think that Civility, wholesome Laws, learning and eloquence, Synods, and Church-maintenance, (that we speak of no more things of this kind) should be as safe as a Sanctuary, and out of shot [εξω βελους];, as they say, that no man would lift up the heel, no, nor dog move his tongue against the motioners of them.[5] For by the first, we are distinguished from brute beasts lead with sensuality; By the second, we are bridled and restrained from outrageous behavior, and from doing of injuries, whether by fraud or by violence; By the third, we are enabled to inform and reform others, by the light and feeling that we have attained unto ourselves; Briefly, by the fourth being brought together to a parley face to face, we sooner compose our differences than by writings which are endless;[6] And lastly, that the Church be sufficiently provided for, is so agreeable to good reason and con-

---

[4] *Having been involved in several translation projects in numerous languages, it is clear that those who feel the burden to produce a Bible translation will often feel the sting of criticism from friend and foe alike.*

[5] *The point is, one would think that religious things would be exempt from the sting of slander. And yet, we find that the opposite is more often than not what is practiced by those who stand against translational work.*

[6] *Attempts were made to discover how many articles and books have been written on the subject of Bible translation in just the English language. When I searched on the phrase "King James Version Controversy" over 33,000,000 hits were registered by the search engine. No doubt, a plethora of opinions have been expressed in varying ways!*

science, that those mothers are holden to be less cruel, that kill their children as soon as they are born, than those nursing fathers and mothers (wheresoever they be) that withdraw from them who hang upon their breasts (and upon whose breasts again themselves do hang to receive the Spiritual and sincere milk of the word) livelihood and support fit for their estates.[7] Thus, it is apparent, that these things which we speak of, are of most necessary use, and therefore, that none, either without absurdity can speak against them, or without note of wickedness can spurn against them.

Yet for all that, the learned know that certain worthy men [Anacharsis with others] have been brought to untimely death for none other fault, but for seeking to reduce their countrymen to good order and discipline; and that in some Commonwealths [e.g. Locri] it was made a capital crime, once to motion the making of a new Law for the abrogating of an old, though the same were most pernicious; And that certain, [Cato the elder], which would be counted pillars of the State, and patterns of Virtue and Prudence, could not be brought for a long time to give way to good Letters and refined speech, but bare themselves as averse from them, as from rocks or boxes of poison; And fourthly, that he was no babe, but a great clerk [Gregory the Divine], that gave forth (and in writing to remain to posterity) in passion peradventure, but yet he gave forth, that he had not seen any profit to come by any Synod, or meeting

---

[7] *This statement seems to be a rebuke against the religious leaders of their day who did not support a new English translation, or, did not support a translation in English in any form. The point is that those who hold this view are like the parent who refuses nourishment to a child that is seeking to be fed.*

of the Clergy, but rather the contrary; And lastly, against Church-maintenance and allowance, in such sort, as the Ambassadors and messengers of the great King of Kings should be furnished, it is not unknown what a fiction or fable (so it is esteemed, and for no better by the reporter himself [Nauclerus], though superstitious) was devised; Namely, that at such a time as the professors and teachers of Christianity in the Church of Rome, then a true Church, were liberally endowed, a voice forsooth was heard from heaven, saying: Now is poison poured down into the Church, etc.[8] Thus, not only as oft as we speak, as one saith, but also as oft as we do anything of note or consequence, we subject ourselves to everyone's censure, and happy is he that is least tossed upon tongues; for utterly to escape the snatch of them it is impossible. If any man conceit, that this is the lot and portion of the meaner sort only, and that Princes are privileged by their high estate, he is deceived. As *the sword devoureth as well one as the other*, as it is in Samuel [2 Sam 11:25], nay as the great Commander charged his soldiers in a certain battle, to strike at no part of the enemy, but at the face; And as the King of Syria commanded his chief Captains *to fight neither with small nor great, save only against the King of Israel:* [1 Kings 22:31] so it is too true, that Envy striketh

---

[8] *This is a reference to a dream that Sylvester, Bishop of Rome (314-335) was said to have had in which he understood his dream to mean "now is poison poured into the church".*

Whether the dream is real or not is subject to debate. But in the mind of the translators, it was an indication that the church had been so poisoned that they were sure to face ridicule for seeking to do a work for the Lord.

most spitefully at the fairest, and at the chiefest.[9] David was a worthy Prince, and no man to be compared to him for his first deeds, and yet for as worthy as act as ever he did (even for bringing back the Ark of God in solemnity) he was scorned and scoffed at by his own wife [2 Sam 6:16]. Solomon was greater than David, though not in virtue, yet in power: and by his power and wisdom he built a Temple to the Lord, such a one as was the glory of the land of Israel, and the wonder of the whole world. But was that his magnificence liked of by all? We doubt of it. Otherwise, why do they lay it in his son's dish, and call unto him for easing of the burden [σεισαχθειαν]: *Make*, say they, *the grievous servitude of thy father, and his sore yoke, lighter.* [1 Kings 12:4] Belike he had charged them with some levies, and troubled them with some carriages; Hereupon they raise up a tragedy, and wish in their heart the Temple had never been built. So hard a thing it is to please all, even when we please God best, and do seek to approve ourselves to everyone's conscience.[10]

---

[9] *It is not that they considered themselves to be great, but the work of translation is a great work. They fully expected their work to be attacked. And so it was in their day. In like fashion, it is still under attack today.*

[10] *The supreme motive for producing a Bible translation ought to be to provide a translation that is an accurate representation of what God gave by inspiration. This is the type of work that will contribute to the edification of man and to the exaltation of our God. Any other motive for translation will not stand the fires of persecution or resistance.*

It is my opinion that many more translations have been started than finished. There is no way to prove it, but in my experience, the ratio has been three to one.

The Highest Personages have been Calumniated[11]

If we will descend to later times, we shall find many the like examples of such kind, or rather unkind acceptance. The first Roman Emperor [C. Caesar, according to Plutarch] did never do a more pleasing deed to the learned, nor more profitable to posterity, for conserving the record of times in true supputation; than when he corrected the Calendar,[12] and ordered the year according to the course of the Sun; and yet this was imputed to him for novelty, and arrogance, and procured to him great obloquy. So, the first Christened Emperor [Constantine][13] (at the leastwise that openly professed the faith himself, and allowed others to do the like) for strengthening the Empire at his great charges, and providing for the Church, as he did, got for his labor the name *Pupillus*, as who would say, a wasteful Prince,

---

[11] *The translators fully expected to be reviled for their work, and, at the time, no doubt there were many who did not appreciate it. Yet now, over 400 years later the King James Version is considered by many to be one of the greatest literary works ever accomplished. And yet, it is still reviled by many.*

[12] *Initially one would think this to be a reference to the Julian calendar which is still in use by the Eastern Orthodox Church today for holidays. Although not strictly ordered by the course of the sun, it was designed by Greek astronomers and mathematicians.*

[13] *I have been involved in numerous discussions where the subject was whether Constantine was a friend or foe to the church. No doubt, Constantine made his mistakes - some with far reaching results. Therefore, it is common among conservative believers to hold Constantine suspect.*

The KJV translators mention Constantine several times. In each instance, he is spoken of with respect. This seems to be their approach to numerous men that we would not appreciate as they did.

that had need of a Guardian or overseer [Aurel. Victor]. So the best Christened Emperor [Theodosius], for the love that he bare unto peace, thereby to enrich both himself and his subjects, and because he did not seek war but find it, was judged to be no man at arms [Zosimus], (though indeed he excelled in feats of chivalry, and showed so much when he was provoked) and condemned for giving himself to his ease, and to his pleasure. To be short, the most learned Emperor of former times [Justinian] (at the least, the greatest politician), what thanks had he for cutting off the superfluities of the laws, and digesting them into some order and method? This, that he hath been blotted by some to be an Epitomist, that is, one that extinguished worthy whole volumes, to bring his abridgments into request. This is the measure that hath been rendered to excellent Princes in former times, even, *Cum bene facerent, male audire,*[14] For their good deeds to be evil spoken of. Neither is there any likelihood, that envy and malignity died, and were buried with the ancient. No, no, the reproof of Moses taketh hold of most ages; *You are risen up in your fathers' stead, an increase of sinful men.* [Num 32:14] *What is that that hath been done? that which shall be done; and there is no new thing under the Sun,* saith the wise man: [Ecc 1:9] and S. Stephen, *As your fathers did, so do you.* [Acts 7:51]

---

[14] *Time and again, throughout the letter, the translators show an uncommon knowledge in many areas, but especially in matters of historical significance. These learned men knew much more than just a few languages or points of deep theology. They were highly educated in a variety of areas.*

His Majesty's Constancy, Notwithstanding Calumniation, for the Survey of the English Translations

This, and more to this purpose, His Majesty that now reigneth (and long, and long may he reign, and his off-spring forever, *"Himself and children, and children's children always"* *["Αυτος, και παιδες, και παιδων παντοτε παιδες"]*) knew full well[15], according to the singular wisdom given unto him by God, and the rare learning and experience that he hath attained unto[16]; namely that whosoever attempts anything for the public (especially if it pertain to Religion, and to the opening and clearing of the word of God) the same sets himself upon a stage to be gloated upon by every evil eye, yea, he casts himself headlong upon pikes, to be gored by every sharp tongue. For he that meddles with men's Religion in any part, meddles with their custom, nay, with their freehold; and though they find no content in that which they have, yet they cannot abide to hear of altering. Notwithstanding his Royal heart was not

---

[15] *It would appear that the translators were aware of the fact that even King James himself understood how authorizing this work would bring contempt upon himself. And this contempt has not ceased to this day. I have read some pretty harsh charges made against King James. The whole motive behind the charges is simply to discredit King James, as if that would be sufficient to discredit the work which he authorized.*

Let the reader remember that whatever may be said of King James himself, he did not do the work of translation, but merely authorized the work to be done.

[16] *King James was given a very extensive education in Greek, French, Latin, classical and religious writings. He was trained by two of the best tutors one could find. King James was well-known to be intellectual, almost to a fault.*

daunted or discouraged for this or that colour, but stood resolute, *as a statue immovable, and an anvil not easy to be beaten into plates* ["ωσπερ τις ανδριασ απεριτρεπτος και ακμων ανη λατος"],, as one [Suidas] saith; he knew who had chosen him to be a Soldier, or rather a Captain, and being assured that the course which he intended made much for the glory of God, and the building up of his Church, he would not suffer it to be broken off for whatsoever speeches or practices. It doth certainly belong unto Kings, yea, it doth specially belong unto them, to have care of Religion[17], yea, it doth specially belong unto them, to have care of Religion, yea, to know it aright, yea, to profess it zealously, yea to promote it to the uttermost of their power. This is their glory before all nations which mean well, and this will bring unto them a far most excellent weight of glory in the day of the Lord Jesus. For the Scripture saith not in vain, *Them that honor me, I will honor,* [1 Sam 2:30] neither was it a vain word that Eu-

---

[17] *These men were certainly not Baptists, believing that the government had a right to moderate religion. And though we may disagree with their conviction on this point, I think the bigger picture had more to do with their charge for the government to promote religion instead of being completely void of it.*

sebius[18] delivered long ago, that piety towards God [θεοσεβεια] was the weapon, and the only weapon, that both preserved Constantine's person, and avenged him of his enemies [Eusebius lib. 10 cap. 8].

The Praise of the Holy Scriptures

But now what piety without truth? what truth (what saving truth) without the word of God? What word of God (whereof we may be sure) without the Scripture?[19] The Scriptures we are commanded to search. John 5:39. Isa 8:20. They are commended that searched and studied them. Acts 17:11 and 8:28,29. They are reproved that were unskillful in them, or slow to believe them. Matt 22:29. Luke 24:25. They can make us wise unto salvation. 2 Tim 3:15. If we be ignorant, they will instruct us; if out of the way, they will bring us home; if out of order, they will reform us; if in heaviness, comfort

---

[18] *Eusebius, a fourth century church historian, and polemist, was at one point given the responsibility by Constantine to produce Greek Bibles of which he produced 50. In doing so, Eusebius noted that there were problems with the Greek texts:*

"If anyone will take the trouble to collect their several copies and compare them, he will discover frequent divergencies; for example, Ascelepiades's copies do not agree with Theodotus's. A large number are obtainable, thanks to the emulous energy with which disciples copied the 'emendations' or rather perversions of the text by their respective masters....it is possible to collate the ones which his disciples made first with those that have undergone further manipulation, and to find endless discrepancies." [Eusebius, The History of the Church from Christ to Constantine, Translated with an introduction by G. A. Williamson. Penguin Books Baltimore, Maryland 1965, p. 237]

[19] *These men were also not Charismatics or Pentecostals (in reality, these movements did not exist yet) seeing they believed that there could be no "word of God" without the Scriptures.*

us; if dull, quicken us; if cold, inflame us. *Tolle, lege; Tolle, lege,* Take up and read, take up and read the Scriptures, (for unto them was the direction) it was said unto S. Augustine[20] by a supernatural voice [S. August. confess. lib 8 cap 12]. *Whatsoever is in the Scriptures, believe me,* saith the same S. Augustine, *is high and divine; there is verily truth, and a doctrine most fit for the refreshing and renewing of men's minds, and truly so tempered, that everyone may draw from thence that which is sufficient for him, if he come to draw with a devout and pious mind, as true Religion requireth [S. August. de utilit. credendi cap. 6].* Thus S. Augustine. And S. Jerome: *Ama scripturas, et amabit te sapientia, etc.* [S. Hieronym. ad Demetriad], "Love the Scriptures, and wisdom will love thee". And S. Cyril against Julian; *Even boys that are bred up in the Scriptures, become most religious, etc.*[S. Cyril. 7o contra Iulianum] But what mention we three or four uses of the Scripture, whereas whatsoever is to be believed or practiced, or hoped for, is contained in them? or three or four sentences of the Fathers, since whosoever is worthy the name of a Father, from Christ's time downward, hath likewise written not only of the riches, but also of the

---

[20] *We know that Augustine believed quite a number of false teachings in varying degrees of seriousness. And so did Jerome. Yet many learned men have read their writings to some extent. Students of religion in the 1600s would have been well-versed in Augustine and Jerome's writings.*

perfection of the Scripture [21]? *I adore the fulness of the Scripture,* saith Tertullian against Hermogenes [Tertul. advers. Hermo.]. And again, to Apelles an heretic of the like stamp, he saith; *I do not admit that which thou bringest in* (or concludest) *of thine own* (head or store, *de tuo*) *without Scripture* [Tertul. de carne Christi]. So Saint Justin Martyr before him; *We must know by all means,* saith he, *that it is not lawful* (or possible) *to learn* (anything) *of God or of right piety, save only out of the Prophets, who teach us by divine inspiration* [Justin προτρεπτ. προς ελλην. οιον τε.] [22]. So Saint Basil after Tertullian, *It is a manifest falling way from the Faith, and a fault of presumption, either to reject any of those things that are written, or to bring in* (upon the head of them, epeisagein) *any of those things that are not written* [S. Basil περι πιστεως. ιπερηφανιας κατηγορια.]. We omit to cite to the same effect, S. Cyril B. of Jerusalem in his fouth *Cataches.*, Saint Jerome against Helvidius, Saint Augustine in his third book against the letters of Petilian, and in very many other places of his works. Also we forebear to descend to later Fathers, because we will not weary the reader. The Scriptures then being acknowledged to be so full and so perfect, how can we excuse ourselves of negligence, if we do

---

[21] *Ah, the perfection of Scripture! These men were not seeking to "recover the originals", as so many so-called scholars of our day say that they are doing. No, these translators believed in the perfection of the Scriptures. And to read what they wrote, it is obvious they believed that they possessed these perfect Scriptures! They certainly did not believe that the true readings had been lost. Nor did they believe that the manuscripts had to be somehow recovered.*

[22] *The translators clearly believed that the Greek and Hebrew were inspired and divinely given of God. They knew that this could never be said of any work of man.*

not study them, of curiosity, if we be not content with them? Men talk much of eiresionae ["Ειρεσιωνη συκα φερει, και πιονας αρτους, και μελιεν κοτυλη, και ελαιον, etc."; an olive bow wrapped about with wood, whereupon did hang figs, and bread, and honey in a pot, and oil], how many sweet and goodly things it had hanging on it; of the Philosopher's stone, that it turns copper into gold; of *Cornucopia*, that it had all things necessary for food in it, of *Panaces* the herb, that it was good for all diseases; of *Catholicon* the drug, that it is instead of all purges; of *Vulcan's* armor, that it was an armor of proof against all thrusts, and all blows, etc. Well, that which they falsely or vainly attributed to these things for bodily good, we may justly and with full measure ascribe unto the Scripture, for spiritual. It is not only an armor, but also a whole armory of weapons, both offensive and defensive; whereby we may save ourselves and put the enemy to flight. It is not an herb, but a tree, or rather a whole paradise of trees of life, which bring forth fruit every month, and the fruit thereof is for meat, and the leaves for medicine. It is not a pot of *Manna*, or a cruse of oil, which were for memory only, or for a meal's meat or two, but as it were a shower of heavenly bread sufficient for a whole host, be it never so great; and as it were a whole cellar full of oil vessels; whereby all our necessities may be provided for, and our debts discharged. In a word, it is a Panary of wholesome food, against fenowed traditions; a Physician's shop (Saint Basil calleth it) ["κοινον ιατρειον.," S. Basil in Psal. primum.] of preservatives against poisoned heresies; a Pandect of profitable laws, against rebellious spirits; a treasury of most costly jewels, against beggarly rudiments; finally a fountain of most pure water springing up unto everlasting life[23]. And what marvel? The original thereof being from heaven, not from earth; the author being God, not man; the indicter, the holy spirit, not the wit of the Apostles or Prophets [24]; the Penmen such as were sanctified from the womb, and endued with a principal portion of God's spirit; the matter, verity, piety, purity, uprightness; the form, God's word, God's testimony, God's oracles, the word of truth, the word of salvation, etc.; the effects, light of understanding, stableness of persuasion, repentance from dead works, newness of life, holiness, peace, joy in the holy Ghost; lastly, the end and reward of the study thereof, fellowship with the Saints, participation of the heavenly nature, fruition of an inheritance immortal, undefiled, and that never shall fade away: Happy is the man that delights in the Scripture, and thrice happy that meditates in it day and night.

---

[23] One cannot read this passage without coming away with the deep impression that these men loved and honored the Bible.

[24] At the very foundation of the modern textual debate is the doctrine of inspiration. These men clearly believe that the Bible was from God. There is not one hint in their writings that they believed the Bible to be merely a religious treatise or that it had become corrupted by men in the process of time.

But how shall men meditate in that, which they cannot understand? How shall they understand that which is kept close in an unknown tongue? as it is written, *Except I know the power of the voice, I shall be to him that speaketh, a Barbarian, and he that speaketh, shall be a Barbarian to me.* [1 Cor 14] The Apostle excepteth no tongue; not Hebrew the ancientest, not Greek the most copious, not Latin the finest. Nature taught a natural man to confess, that all of us in those tongues which we do not understand, are plainly deaf; we may turn the deaf ear unto them. The Scythian counted the Athenian, whom he did not understand, barbarous [Clem. Alex. 1o Strom.]; so the Roman did the Syrian, and the Jew (even S. Jerome himself calleth the Hebrew tongue barbarous, belike because it was strange to so many) [S. Hieronym. Damaso.] so the Emperor of Constantinople [Michael, Theophili fil.] calleth the Latin tongue, barbarous, though Pope Nicolas do storm at it [2 Tom. Concil. ex edit. Petri Crab.]; so the Jews long before Christ called all other nations, *Lognazim*, which is little better than barbarous. Therefore as one complaineth, that always in the Senate of Rome, there was one or other that called for an interpreter [Cicero 5o de

---

25 *What could be done for a person who has no Bible to read, to help them to grow, to be encouraged, to seek direction? The oratory ability of men may be nice but the pure Word of God is essential. The work of Bible translation is the "first necessity" in order for true mission work to be accomplished. For this very reason, many translations have been accomplished in thousands of languages over the course of history. Some of these translations were very base. But putting myself in a missionary's shoes, what else could we expect but that a missionary would do his very best to put the Scriptures into the hands of the people he loved?*

finibus.], so lest the Church be driven to the like exigent, it is necessary to have translations in a readiness. translation it is that openeth the window, to let in the light; that breaketh the shell, that we may eat the kernel; that putteth aside the curtain, that we may look into the most Holy place; that removeth the cover of the well, that we may come by the water, even as Jacob rolled away the stone from the mouth of the well, by which means the flocks of Laban were watered [Gen 29:10]. Indeed without translation[26] into the vulgar tongue, the unlearned are but like children at Jacob's well (which was deep) [John 4:11] without a bucket or something to draw with; or as that person mentioned by Isaiah, to whom when a sealed book was delivered, with this motion, *Read this, I pray thee,* he was fain to make this answer, *I cannot, for it is sealed.* [Isa 29:11]

The Translation of the Old Testament out of the Hebrew into Greek

While God would be known only in Jacob, and have his Name great in Israel, and in none other place, while the dew lay on Gideon's fleece only, and all the earth besides was dry; then for one and the same people, which spake all of them the language of Canaan, that is, Hebrew, one and the same original in Hebrew was suffi-

---

[26] *As much as we know that inspiration is not a quality that resides in a translation, (or even in the original writing itself) but a process by which God delivered His words to man; and preservation is the divine intervention of God to ensure no word or thought is corrupted or lost, we still recognize and readily admit that without translation, millions would still be unable to comprehend the Word of God. There is no light without understanding. For if a trumpet give an uncertain sound, who shall prepare himself to the battle? (1 Cor 14:8)*

cient [S. August. lib. 12 contra Faust. c. 32]. But, when the fulness of time drew near, that the Sun of righteousness, the Son of God should come into the world, whom God ordained to be a reconciliation through faith in his blood, not of the Jew only, but also of the Greek, yea, of all them that were scattered abroad; then lo, it pleased the Lord to stir up the spirit of a Greek Prince (Greek for descent and language) even of Ptolemy Philadelph King of Egypt[27], to procure the translating of the Book of God out of Hebrew into Greek. This is the translation of the Seventy Interpreters, commonly so called, which prepared the way for our Saviour among the Gentiles[28] by written preaching, as Saint John Baptist did among the Jews by vocal. For the Grecians being desirous of learning, were not wont to suffer books of worth to lie moulding in Kings' libraries, but had many of their servants, ready scribes, to copy them out, and so they were dispersed and made common. Again, the Greek tongue was well known and made familiar to most inhabitants in Asia, by reason of the conquest that there the Grecians had made, as also by the Colonies, which thither they had sent. For the same causes also,

---

[27] *The translators obviously believed the story concerning the creation of the Septuagint. Those who question its existence in the first century would have a hard time using the KJV translators' statements to justify their positions. In my opinion, it is incredibly hypocritical to exemplify the translators with comments like, "Do you really think you know more than the KJV translators? They were the greatest group of translators ever assembled. They could speak forty-eleven languages... blab, blab, blab..." and then turn right around and say that they didn't know what they were talking about when it comes to the Septuagint.*

[28] *The translators believed that the Septuagint was the translation used to take the gospel to the Gentiles. And this makes sense seeing that Greek is a language the Gentiles could understand.*

it was well understood in many places of Europe, yea, and of Africa too. Therefore, the word of God being set forth in Greek, becometh hereby like a candle set upon a candlestick, which giveth light to all that are in the house, or like a proclamation sounded forth in the market place, which most men presently take knowledge of; and therefore, that language was fittest to contain the Scriptures, both for the first Preachers of the Gospel to appeal unto for witness, and for the learners also of those times to make search and trial by. It is certain, that that translation was not so sound and so perfect, but that it needed in many places correction[29]; and who had been so sufficient for this work as the Apostles or Apostolic men? Yet it seemed good to the holy Ghost and to them, to take that which they found, (the same being for the greatest part true and sufficient) rather than by making a new, in that new world and green age of the Church, to expose themselves to many exceptions and cavillations, as though they made a translation to serve their own turn, and therefore bearing witness to themselves, their witness not to be regarded. This may be supposed to be some cause, why the translation of the Seventy was allowed to pass for current[30]. Notwithstanding, though it was commended

---

[29] *There is no doubt that the Septuagint was a translation with its own set of problems in many areas that needed correction. The translators were quite aware of this. Yet in reading this, the translators certainly believed that the apostles used it in their ministries among the Greek speaking Jews (Grecians) as well as among the Gentiles.*

[30] *The argument that the Septuagint did not really exist until the time of Origen is not one that the KJV translators would agree with. They clearly speak of it as not only being current but also in use.*

generally, yet it did not fully content the learned[31], no not of the Jews. For not long after Christ, Aquila fell in hand with a new translation, and after him Theodotion, and after him Symmachus; yea, there was a fifth and a sixth edition, the Authors whereof were not known. These with the Seventy made up the *Hexapla* and were worthily and to great purpose compiled together by Origen.[32] Howbeit the Edition of the Seventy went away with the credit, and therefore not only was placed in the midst by Origen (for the worth and excellency thereof above the rest, as Epiphanius gathered [Epiphan. de mensur. et ponderibus.]) but also was used by the Greek fathers for the ground and foundation of their Commentaries. Yea, Epiphanius above named doth at-

---

[31] *Keep in mind that the translators were not seeking to defend, nor attack, the Septuagint. They knew that there were problems with it. But they still considered it a worthy work.*

[32] *It is not uncommon to hear defenders of the King James speak very poorly of Origen. The translators did not take that approach. Again, Origen had his theological issues. But anyone schooled in theology would have been familiar with his works.*

I would also like to point out that the KJV translators make no mention of a common theory I hear today. I keep hearing that Origen actually changed the Septuagint to match New Testament readings. Yet, as far as I can see, there is no real evidence for this position. In fact, it would seem easier to prove otherwise.

The basis for this theory is because the New Testament writers, who wrote in Greek, when quoting the Old Testament, often use phraseology identical to the Septuagint. Since we know that the Septuagint is an inferior translation, there are those who are not comfortable with the thought that the New Testament writers would have used such an inferior translation.

In order to alleviate the problem, someone (and I don't really know who was first) has propagated the theory that Origen edited the Septuagint to match the New Testament Greek manuscripts.

tribute so much unto it, that he holdeth the Authors thereof not only for Interpreters, but also for Prophets in some respect; and Justinian the Emperor enjoining the Jews his subjects to use especially the translation of the Seventy, rendereth this reason thereof, because they were as it were enlightened with prophetical grace [S. August. 2o de doctrin. Christian. c. 15o. Novell. di-atax. 146]. Yet for all that, as the Egyptians are said of the Prophet to be men and not God, and their horses flesh and not spirit [προφητικης ωσπερ χαριτος περιλαμψασης αυτους, Isa. 31:3]; so it is evident, (and Saint Jerome affirmeth as much) [S. Hieron. de optimo genero interpret.] that the Seventy were Inter-preters, they were not Prophets[33]; they did many things well, as learned men; but yet as men they stumbled and fell, one while through oversight, another while through ignorance, yea, sometimes they may be noted to add to the Original, and sometimes to take from it [34]; which made the Apostles to leave them many times, when they left the Hebrew, and to deliver the sense thereof according to the truth of the word, as the spirit

---

[33] *There is a legend that the translators of the Septuagint were isolated from one another and worked independently. And yet, according to the legend, when they came together to compare their work, all of their work was identical. Again, this is purely legend. But it was believed by enough Jewish scholars to propagate another legendary belief that the translators were inspired. Clearly, the KJV translators did not hold this same opinion. They did not hold to the false belief of double inspiration, or, advanced revelation.*

[34] *The translators mention several problems with the Septuagint. In doing so, they also indirectly warn all Bible translators of areas to be most careful in - oversight, ignorance, adding to the original, taking away from the original.*

gave them utterance[35]. This may suffice touching the Greek translations of the Old Testament.

Translation out of Hebrew and Greek into Latin

There were also within a few hundred years after Christ, translations many into the Latin tongue: for this tongue also was very fit to convey the Law and the Gospel by, because in those times very many Countries of the West, yea of the South, East and North, spake or understood Latin, being made Provinces to the Romans. But now the Latin translations were too many to be all good, for they were infinite (*Latini Interpretes nullo modo numerari possunt*, saith S. Augustine) [S. Augustin. de doctr. Christ. lib. 2 cap. 11]. Again they were not out of the Hebrew fountain (we speak of the Latin translations of the Old Testament) but out of the Greek

---

[35] *Much argumentation has been put forth concerning the differences and similarities in the New Testament Greek manuscripts as compared to the Septuagint. The KJV translators believed that in a number of places, the apostles did not mean to quote from the Septuagint at all. But knowing that there were translational problems, they "gave the sense". But let's not forget that the apostles were also inspired by the Spirit to write as they did and had perfect liberty to record the message as the Spirit moved them. Those who believe in verbal-plenary inspiration should not be troubled by these differences.*

stream[36]. Therefore the Greek being not altogether clear, the Latin derived from it must needs be muddy. This moved S. Jerome a most learned father, and the best linguist without controversy, of his age, or of any that went before him, to undertake the translating of the Old Testament, out of the very fountains themselves, which he performed with that evidence of great learning, judgment, industry, and faithfulness, that he hath forever bound the Church unto him, in a debt of special remembrance and thankfulness [37].

---

[36] *The translators are addressing two problems here at the same time. First, an overabundance of translations of the Old Testament in Latin, and second, that many were not translated directly from the Hebrew but from a Greek translation of the Hebrew.*

This is reminiscent of two problems we have in modern English today. First, there are so many English translations and almost as many opinions on which is best. Second, there is a movement afoot that it is not just acceptable, but almost preferred: to translate directly from the **inspired** *KJV (or* **preserved** *KJV, or* **perfect** *KJV). But it is clear that the KJV translators believed in direct translation from Greek and Hebrew. They did not think it best to produce a translation of a translation.*

I am not saying that it is wrong to translate directly from the KJV. In many cases, a missionary may have little to no other option. It is not wrong, but certainly not the preferred method.

[37] *Whereas it seems almost in vogue to speak disparagingly of scholars and linguists who have gone before us, I do not think that the KJV translators would share this opinion. In Jerome's case, he has been accused of doing a shoddy translation, of being an enemy of the church, and so on.*

But the KJV translators called him "a most learned father, and the best linguist without controversy, of his age, or of any that went before him".

The Translating of the Scripture into the Vulgar Tongues

Now though the Church were thus furnished with Greek and Latin translations, even before the faith of Christ was generally embraced in the Empire[38]; (for the learned know that even in S. Jerome's time, the Consul of Rome and his wife were both Ethnics, and about the same time the greatest part of the Senate also)[S. Hieronym. Marcell. Zosim]; yet for all that the godly-learned were not content to have the Scriptures in the Language which themselves understood, Greek and Latin, (as the good Lepers were not content to fare well themselves, but acquainted their neighbors with the store that God had sent, that they also might provide for themselves) [2 Kings 7:9] but also for the behoof and edifying of the unlearned which hungered and thirsted after righteousness, and had souls to be saved as well as they, they provided translations into the vulgar for their Countrymen[39], insomuch that most nations under

---

[38] *In the words of the KJV translators, translation work was already in progress even before the gospel was "embraced in the Empire". Therefore, we should not be surprised to find the existence of a variety of translations predating the Edict of Constantine which made Christianity legal in the Roman Empire.*

[39] *Let me reiterate a point made earlier. A missionary on the field has a primary responsibility to put the Word of God in the language of those that he is seeking to reach. The time will come that the missionary will leave the field or pass on into glory. But the Word of God will be the one thing that sustains the people after the missionary is gone.*

Additionally, it ought to be the burden of every minister of the gospel to see his people reading the Bible, and learning from the Lord, for themselves. This demands that a translation be done if there is none, and a better translation be done if what exists is lacking.

heaven did shortly after their conversion, hear Christ speaking unto them in their mother tongue, not by the voice of their Minister only, but also by the written word translated. If any doubt hereof, he may be satisfied by examples enough, if enough will serve the turn. First S. Jerome saith, *Multarum gentium linguis Scriptura ante translata, docet falsa esse quae addita sunt, etc. i.e. The Scripture being translated before in the languages of many Nations, doth show that those things that were added* (by Lucian or Hesychius) *are false* [S. Hieron. praef. in 4. Evangel.]. So S. Jerome in that place. The same Jerome elsewhere affirmeth that he, the time was, had set forth the translation of the Seventy, *suae linguae hominibus*, i.e., for his countrymen of Dalmatia [S. Hieron. Sophronio.]. Which words not only Erasmus doth understand to purport, that S. Jerome translated the Scripture into the Dalmatian tongue, but also Sixtus Senensis [Six. Sen. lib. 4] and Alphonsus a Castro [Alphon. a' Castro lib. 1 ca. 23] (that we speak of no more) men not to be excepted against by them of Rome, do ingenuously confess as much. So, S. Chrysostom that lived in S. Jerome's time, giveth evidence with him: *The doctrine of S. John* (saith he) *did not in such sort* (as the Philosophers' did) *vanish away: but the Syrians, Egyptians, Indians, Persians, Ethiopians, and infinite other nations being barbarous people translated it into their (mother) tongue, and have learned to be (true) Philosophers,* he meaneth Christians [S. Chrysost. in Johan. cap. hom. 1]. To this may be added Theodoret, as next unto him, both for antiquity, and for learning. His words be these, *Every Country that is under the Sun, is full of these words* (of the Apostles and Prophets) *and the Hebrew tongue* (he meaneth the Scriptures in the Hebrew tongue) *is turned not only into the Language of the Grecians, but also of the Romans, and Egyptians, and Persians, and Indians, and Armenians, and Scythians, and Sauromatians, and briefly into all the Languages that any Nation useth* [Theodor. 5. Therapeut.] [40]. So he. In like manner, Ulfilas is reported by Paulus Diaconus and Isidor (and before them by Sozomen) to have translated the Scriptures into the Gothic tongue [P. Diacon. lib. 12, Isidor in Chron. Goth, Sozom. lib. 6 cap. 37]: John Bishop of Sevil by Vasseus, to have turned them into Arabic, about the year of our Lord 717 [Vaseus in Chron. Hispan.]; Bede by Cistertiensis, to have turned a great part of them into Saxon [Polydor Virg. 5 histor. Anglorum testatur idem de Alvredo nostro]: Efnard by Trithemius, to have abridged the French Psalter, as Bede had done the Hebrew, about the year 800: King Alfred by the said Cistertiensis, to have turned the Psalter into Saxon: Methodius by Aventinus (printed at Ingolstadt) to have turned the Scriptures into Slavonian [Aventin. lib. 4.]: Valdo, Bishop of Frising by Beatus Rhenanus, to have caused about that time, the Gospels to be translated into Dutch rhythm, yet extant in the Library of Corbinian [Circa annum 900. B. Rhenan. rerum German. lib 2.]: Valdus, by divers to have turned them himself, or to have gotten them turned, into French, about the year 1160: Charles the Fifth of that name, surnamed the Wise, to have caused them to be turned into French, about 200 years after Valdus his time, of which translation there be many copies yet extant, as witnesseth

---

[40] *From the testimony of those who lived during the time period of which they spoke, the Bible had been translated into quite a number of languages. Many of these translations have passed into antiquity.*

Beroaldus. Much about that time, even in our King Richard the second's days, John Trevisa[41] translated them into English, and many English Bibles in written hand are yet to be seen with divers, translated as it is very probable, in that age. So the Syrian translation of the New Testament is in most learned men's Libraries, of Widminstadius his setting forth, and the Psalter in Arabic is with many, of Augustinus Nebiensis' setting forth. So Postel affirmeth, that in his travel he saw the Gospels in the Ethiopian tongue; And Ambrose Thesius allegeth the Pslater of the Indians, which he testifieth to have been set forth by Potken in Syrian characters. So that, to have the Scriptures in the mother tongue is not a quaint conceit lately taken up, either by the Lord Cromwell in England, or by the Lord Radevile in Polony [Thuan.], or by the Lord Ungnadius in the Emperor's dominion, but hath been thought upon, and put in practice of old, even from the first times of the conversion of any Nation[42]; no doubt, because it was esteemed most profitable, to cause faith to grow in men's hearts the sooner, and to make them to be able to say with the

---

[41] *John Trevisa's English translation is unknown. As a result, it is thought that he was a contributor to the Wycliffe translation. We know that he also translated parts of the Bible into French for Lord Berkeley as well.*

[42] *The translators' knowledge of translations in history is exceptional. Many of the works to which they refer are rarely, if ever, spoken of in history nor theology books today. One could glean much about the history of Bible translations just by reading the letter of the translators to the readers.*

words of the Psalm, *As we have heard, so we have seen.* [Ps 48:8][43]

The Unwillingness of Our Chief Adversaries, that the Scriptures Should Be Divulged in the Mother Tongue, etc.

Now the Church of Rome would seem at the length to bear a motherly affection towards her children, and to allow them the Scriptures in their mother tongue: but indeed it is a gift, not deserving to be called a gift, an unprofitable gift [δωρον αδωρον κουκ ονησιμον, Sophocles]: they must first get a license in writing before they may use them, and to get that, they must approve themselves to their Confessor, that is, to be such as are, if not frozen in the dregs, yet soured with the leaven of their superstition[44]. Howbeit, it seemed too much to Clement the Eighth that there should be any License granted to have them in the vulgar tongue, and therefore he overruleth and frustrateth the grant of Pius the Fourth [See the observation (set forth by Clement his authority) upon the fourth rule of Pius the Fourth his making in the Index, lib. prohib., pag. 15. ver. 5.] [45]. So much are they afraid of the light of the Scripture, (*Lu-*

---

[43] *Having the Word of God in one's mother tongue, as some would say, their heart language, is very beneficial to the growth of a person's faith. The KJV Translators understood this quite clearly.*

[44] *In other words, the only people would could get a license, which in itself is deplorable, were those who were known to have already been thoroughly corrupted by false Catholic doctrine.*

[45] *Pius the Fourth had originally allowed for translational work into English apparently. But later, Clement the Eighth would have none of it.*

cifugae Scripturarum, as Tertulian speaketh [Tertul. de resur. carnis]) that they will not trust the people with it, no not as it is set forth by their own sworn men, no not with the license of their own bishops and inquisitors. Yea, so unwilling they are to communicate the Scriptures to the people's understanding in any sort, that they are not ashamed to confess, that we forced them to translate it into English against their wills. This seemeth to argue a bad cause, or a bad conscience, or both. Sure we are, that it is not he that hath good gold, that is afraid to bring it to the touchstone, but he that hath the counterfeit; neither is it the true man that shunneth the light, but the malefactor, lest his deeds should be reproved [John 3:20]: neither is it the plain-dealing Merchant that is unwilling to have the weights, or the meteyard brought in place, but he that useth deceit[46]. But we will let them alone for this fault, and return to translation.

The Speeches and Reasons, both of Our Brethren, and of Our Adversaries against this Work

Many men's mouths have been open a good while (and yet are not stopped) with speeches about the translation so long in hand, or rather perusals of translations made before: and ask what may be the reason, what the necessity of the employment: Hath the Church been

---

[46] *The translators believed that the sole reason that the Catholic Church did not want the Scriptures in the common language was because the light of the Scriptures would reveal their false doctrines.*

deceived, say they, all this while[47]? Hath her sweet bread been mingled with leaven, her silver with dross, her wine with water, her milk with lime? (*Lacte gypsum male miscetur*, saith S. Ireney [S. Iren. 3. lib. cap. 19.].) We hoped that we had been in the right way, that we had had the Oracles of God delivered unto us, and that though all the world had cause to be offended and to complain, yet that we had none. Hath the nurse holden out the breast, and nothing but wind in it? Hath the bread been delivered by the fathers of the Church, and the same proved to be *lapidosus*, as Seneca speaketh? What is it to handle the word of God deceitfully, if this be not? Thus certain brethren. Also the adversaries of Judah and Jerusalem, like Sanballat in Nehemiah, mock, as we hear, both at the work and workmen, saying; *What do these weak Jews, etc. will they make the stones whole again out of the heaps of dust which are burnt? although they build, yet if a fox go up, he shall even break down their stony wall.* [Neh 4:3] Was their translation good before? Why do they now mend it? Was it not good? Why then was it obtruded to the people[48]? Yea, why did the Catholics (meaning Popish

---

[47] *In other words, "What is the need of a new translation when the old has served the purpose for so long?" I have actually been involved with a translation project where a good translation already existed but needed to be made better. One of the arguments against the translation project was exactly this. The translators show us by example that if improvements can be made, then improvements should be made.*

[48] *In any language where a good translation exists, souls are saved, churches are built, believers are edified, and Christ is exalted. Yet, the knowledge that it is possible to make a good translation better should motivate those who have the skills of language to do it. This is why there are Bible translation projects under way world-wide in languages where a previous translation already exists.*

Romanists) always go in jeopardy, for refusing to go to hear it? Nay, if it must be translated into English, Catholics are fittest to do it. They have learning, and they know when a thing is well, they can *manum de tabula*[49]. We will answer them both briefly: and the former, being brethren, thus, with S. Jerome, *Damnamus veteres? Mineme, sed post priorum studia in domo Domini quod possums laboramus* [S. Hieron. Apolog. advers. Ruffin.]. That is, *Do we condemn the ancient? In no case: but after the endeavors of them that were before us, we take the best pains we can in the house of God.* As if he said, Being provoked by the example of the learned that lived before my time, I have thought it my duty, to assay whether my talent in the knowledge of the tongues[50], may be profitable in any measure to God's Church, lest I should seem to have labored in them in vain, and lest I should be thought to glory in

---

[49] *Let me be perfectly clear. It takes more than education to produce a good translator. The work also requires a high level of piety for the translator will undoubtedly need to call upon the wisdom and guidance of the Holy Spirit in many situations. This would have been impossible for the Catholics who do know the truth of salvation by faith alone.*

Then, moving forward to the late 1800s, this was also a major flaw in having irreligious men such as Westcott and Hort handling the Scriptures. Truly they handled the Word of God deceitfully.

[50] *The language ability of these men was astonishing by today's standards. Most spoke, read and wrote multiple languages fluently. All of the translators were skilled in Hebrew and Greek. Add to this the knowledge of most of the languages of Europe, Ethiopic languages, Aramaic, Coptic, Persian, Arabic, Latin, as well as others. Lancelot Andrews spoke 15 languages fluently. Miles Smith spoke four languages so fluently that they were as familiar to him as his own mother tongue. John Bois is said to have read the Bible in Hebrew by the age of five and could turn to any Greek word in the New Testament upon request - a literal walking Greek concordance!*

men, (although ancient,) above that which was in them. Thus S. Jerome may be thought to speak.

A Satisfaction to Our Brethren

And to the same effect say we, that we are so far off from condemning any of their labors that travailed before us in this kind, either in this land or beyond sea, either in King Henry's time, or King Edward's (if there were any translation, or correction of a translation in his time) or Queen Elizabeth's of ever renowned memory, that we acknowledge them to have been raised up of God, for the building and furnishing of his Church, and that they deserve to be had of us and of posterity in everlasting remembrance[51]. The judgment of Aristotle is worthy and well known: *If Timotheus had not been, we had not had much sweet music; but if Phrynis* (Timotheus his master) *had not been, we had not had Timotheus* [Arist. 2 metaphys. cap. 1]. Therefore blessed be they, and most honored be their name, that break the ice, and giveth onset upon that which helpeth forward

---

[51] *Some would point out that the KJV translators did not condemn the other translations even though they were inferior. Then they go a step further to assert that the KJV translators would not condemn the translations of today.*

*But two things must be kept in mind. First of all, the KJV translators lived well before the creation of the Critical Text and thus were speaking **only** of Textus Receptus-based or Byzantine-based translations.*

Secondly, it is extremely presumptuous to assume that we know what the translators of 1611 would think about some of the methods employed in translation today. Whereas they held to a formal equivalent (word-for-word) philosophy, most of the modern translations are based on a dynamic equivalency (the main idea) philosophy. I seriously doubt the KJV translators would have agreed to that.

to the saving of souls[52]. Now what can be more available thereto, than to deliver God's book unto God's people in a tongue which they understand? Since of a hidden treasure, and of a fountain that is sealed, there is no profit, as Ptolemy Philadelph wrote to the Rabbins or masters of the Jews, as witnesseth Epiphanius [S. Epiphan. loco ante citato]: and as S. Augustine saith; *A man had rather be with his dog than with a stranger* (whose tongue is strange unto him) [S. Augustin. lib. 19. de civit. Dei. c. 7.]. Yet for all that, as nothing is begun and perfected at the same time, and the later thoughts are thought to be the wiser: so, if we building upon their foundation that went before us, and being holpen by their labors, do endeavor to make that better which they left so good[53]; no man, we are sure, hath cause to mislike us; they, we persuade ourselves, if they were alive, would thank us. The vintage of Abiezer, that strake the stroke: yet the gleaning of grapes of Ephraim was not to be despised. (see Judges 8:2). Joash the king of Israel did not satisfy himself, till he had smitten the ground three times; and yet he offended the Prophet, for giving over then. [2 Kings 13:18-19] Aquila, of whom we spoke before, translated the Bible as carefully, and as skillfully as he could; and yet he thought good to go over it again, and then it got the credit with the Jews, to be called kata akribeian, that is,

---

[52] *They recognized that it would be wrong to disdain that which came before them for that which came before them helped to mold them so that they could do further work.*

[53] *The great difference between these men and modern translators is that modern translator's approach from a completely different textual base and with completely different translational philosophies. Thus, they cannot truly say they are building upon an earlier work.*

accurately done, as Saint Jerome witnesseth [S. Jerome. in Ezech. cap. 3.]. How many books of profane learning have been gone over again and again, by the same translators, by others[54]? Of one and the same book of Aristotle's *Ethics*, there are extant not so few as six or seven several translations. Now if this cost may be bestowed upon the gourd, which affordeth us a little shade, and which today flourisheth, but tomorrow is cut down; what may we bestow, nay what ought we not to bestow upon the Vine, the fruit whereof maketh glad the conscience of man, and the stem whereof abideth forever? And this is the word of God, which we translate. *What is the chaff to the wheat, saith the Lord?* [Jer 23:28] *Tanti vitreum, quanti verum margaritum* (saith Tertullian, [Tertul. ad Martyr.]) if a toy of glass be of that reckoning with us, how ought we to value the true pearl [Si tanti vilissimum vitrium, quanti pretiosissimum margaritum, Hieron. ad Salvin.]? Therefore let no man's eye be evil, because his Majesty's is good; neither let any be grieved, that we have a Prince that seeketh the increase of the spiritual wealth of Israel (let Sanballats and Tobiahs do so, which therefore do bear their just reproof) but let us rather bless God from the ground of our heart, for working this religious care in him, to have the translations of the Bible maturely considered of and examined. For by this means it cometh to pass, that

---

[54] *The KJV translators, in this section, are defending the fact that they would be correcting upon English translations that went before them. They did not intend to, nor does it appear, that they began from scratch. There are many similarities between the KJV and some of the English translations that came before it.*

And we would expect this to be the case seeing that one would not want to change what was already correct and accepted.

whatsoever is sound already (and all is sound for substance, in one or other of our editions, and the worst of ours far better than their authentic vulgar) the same will shine as gold more brightly, being rubbed and polished; also, if anything be halting, or superfluous, or not so agreeable to the original[55], the same may be corrected, and the truth set in place. And what can the King command to be done, that will bring him more true honor than this? and wherein could they that have been set a work, approve their duty to the King, yea their obedience to God, and love to his Saints more, than by yielding their service, and all that is within them, for the furnishing of the work[56]? But besides all this, they were the principal motives of it, and therefore ought least to quarrel it: for the very Historical truth is, that upon the importunate petitions of the Puritans, at his Majesty's

---

[55] *The KJV Translators actually encouraged others to follow after them and correct any mistake that they may have made insofar as what they did conflicted with the original languages. In studying the history of the KJV, this type of work has been done, the first two revisions in 1629 and 1638. The final changes being accomplished in 1769. The majority of the changes constituted spelling updates and grammatical changes.*

Even Thomas Nelson Publishers admits that the changes from 1611 to 1769 could by no means be considered extensive, stating, "On the surface, it may seem as though the 1611 edition has undergone an extensive overhaul. But that's not necessarily the case. The essence of the original King James Version remains intact today. If you were to compare a current edition of the text to the original, you would find that they are remarkably similar." (www.thomasnelson.com)

[56] *We should note that the men that were involved in the translation work were an assembly of the greatest scholars of their time. And yet, except for the mention of their names in the annals of history, they would have been largely unknown except that they took upon themselves to translate the greatest book of all time. And in doing so, they produced the greatest translation of all time. For this, they are well-remembered.*

coming to this Crown, the Conference at Hampton Court having been appointed for hearing their complaints: when by force of reason they were put from all other grounds, they had recourse at the last, to this shift, that they could not with good conscience subscribe to the Communion book, since it maintained the Bible as it was there translated, which was as they said, a most corrupted translation[57]. And although this was judged to be but a very poor and empty shift; yet even hereupon did his Majesty begin to bethink himself of the good that might ensue by a new translation, and presently after gave order for this translation which is now presented unto thee. Thus much to satisfy our scrupulous Brethren.

An Answer to the Imputations of Our Adversaries

Now to the latter we answer; that we do not deny, nay we affirm and avow, that the very meanest translation of the Bible in English, set forth by men of our profession, (for we have seen none of theirs of the whole Bible as yet) containeth the word of God, nay, is the

---

[57] *The Communion book to which they referred was the book of Common Prayer, which in their time contained the English translation of the Great Bible (Geneva Bible). It is commonly believed that the Puritans liked the Geneva Bible. So, either the text was corrupted somehow as it was placed into the Book of Common Prayer, or else, there were those who were not as fond of it as we think they were.*

word of God[58]. As the King's speech, which he uttereth in Parliament, being translated into French, Dutch, Italian, and Latin, is still the King's speech, though it be not interpreted by every Translator with the like grace, nor peradventure so fitly for phrase, nor so expressly for sense, everywhere. For it is confessed, that things are to take their denomination of the greater part; and a natural man could say, *Verum ubi multa nitent in carmine, non ego paucis offendor maculis, etc.*[Horace] A man may be counted a virtuous man, though he have made many slips in his life, (else, there were none virtuous, for *in many things we offend all*) [James 3:2] also a comely man and lovely, though he have some warts upon his hand, yea, not only freckles upon his face, but also scars. No cause therefore why the word translated should be denied to be the word, or forbidden to be current, notwithstanding that some imperfections and blemishes may be noted in the setting forth of it[59]. For what ever was perfect under the Sun, where Apostles or Apostolic men, that is, men endued with an extraordinary measure of God's spirit, and privileged with

---

[58] *Now, here is a statement that would get the translators booted from many of our churches today. They believed that it was perfectly acceptable to call a less-than-perfect translation the Word of God. It may not be as exact as it should have been, but it still conveys the message of the King. That being said, I wonder if they would feel the same if they knew that so many translations today use a completely different Greek text than what they used?*

[59] *Interestingly, the KJV translators did not claim perfection in their work, though many today do. In fact, by including alternate possible translations, they were basically admitting that they had reservations in some points as to whether they had chosen the right word or not.*

the privilege of infallibility, had not their hand[60]? The Romanists therefore in refusing to hear, and daring to burn the Word translated, did no less than despite the spirit of grace, from whom originally it proceeded, and whose sense and meaning, as well as man's weakness would enable, it did express. Judge by an example or two. Plutarch writeth, that after that Rome had been burnt by the Gauls, they fell soon to build it again: but doing it in haste, they did not cast the streets, nor proportion the houses in such comely fashion, as had been most sightly and convenient [Plutarch in Camillo.]; was Catiline therefore an honest man, or a good patriot, that sought to bring it to a combustion? or Nero a good Prince, that did indeed set it on fire? So, by the story of Ezra, and the prophecy of Haggai it may be gathered, that the Temple built by Zerubbabel after the return from Babylon, was by no means to be compared to the former built by Solomon (for they that remembered the former, wept when they considered the latter) [Ezra 3:12] notwithstanding, might this latter either have been abhorred and forsaken by the Jews, or profaned by the Greeks? The like we are to think of translations[61]. The translation of the Seventy dissenteth from the Original in many places, neither doth it come near it, for perspicuity, gravity, majesty; yet which of the Apostles did

---

[60] *Translators are not endued with the power of the Spirit in the same fashion that the original writers were. Translators can claim no added insight or inspiration in their translations.*

[61] *In their opinion, not only are other translations the word of God and ought to be honored as such, even translations of lower quality ought to be so regarded.*

condemn it? Condemn it? Nay, they used it[62], (as it is apparent, and as Saint Jerome and most learned men do confess) which they would not have done, nor by their example of using it, so grace and commend it to the Church, if it had been unworthy the appellation and name of the word of God. And whereas they urge for their second defense of their vilifying and abusing of the English Bibles, or some pieces thereof, which they meet with, for that heretics (forsooth) were the Authors of the translations, (heretics they call us by the same right that they call themselves Catholics, both being wrong) we marvel what divinity taught them so. We are sure Tertullian was of another mind: *Ex personis probamus fidem, an ex fide personas?* [Tertul. de praescript. contra haereses.] Do we try men's faith by their persons? we should try their persons by their faith. Also S. Augustine was of another mind: for he lighting upon certain rules made by Tychonius a Donatist, for the better understanding of the word, was not ashamed to make use of them[63], yea, to insert them into his own book, with giving commendation to them so far forth as they were worthy to be commended, as is to be seen in S. Augustine's third book *De doctrina Christiana* [S. August. 3. de doct. Christ. cap. 30.]. To be short, Origen,

---

[62] *The KJV scholars, the most learned men of their time, believed that the Septuagint was actually used by the apostles. Why would so many deny this today except that they are uncomfortable with the thought that they used a translation so clearly inferior? But if not the Septuagint, then what did Paul use among the Gentiles who by and large could not have known Hebrew?*

[63] *Here is an interesting point. It is a fact of history that Augustine, a friend of supporter of the Catholic Church, had a disdain for the Donatists, even speaking out against them. But he had the sense to accept something from the Donatists that he believed was valid and true.*

and the whole Church of God for certain hundred years, were of another mind: for they were so far from treading under foot, (much more from burning) the translation of Aquila a Proselyte, that is, one that had turned Jew; of Symmachus, and Theodotion, both Ebionites, that is, most vile heretics, that they joined them together with the Hebrew Original, and the translation of the Seventy (as hath been before signified out of Epiphanius) and set them forth openly to be considered of and perused by all[64]. But we weary the unlearned, who need not know so much, and trouble the learned, who know it already.

Yet before we end, we must answer a third cavil and objection of theirs against us, for altering and amending our translations so oft; wherein truly they deal hardly,

---

[64] *So, what was their underlying point? Simply that we need not to commend everything about a source in order to recognize when that source produces something good.*

and strangely with us[65]. For to whom ever was it imputed for a fault (by such as were wise) to go over that which he had done, and to amend it where he saw cause[66]? Saint Augustine was not afraid to exhort S. Jerome to a *Palinodia* or recantation; the same S. Augustine was not ashamed to retractate, we might say revoke, many things that had passed him, and doth even glory that he seeth his infirmities [S. Aug. Epist. 9; S. Aug. lib. Retractat.; Video interdum vitia mea, S. Aug. Epist. 8.]. If we will be sons of the Truth, we must consider what it speaketh, and trample upon our own credit, yea, and upon other men's too, if either be any

---

[65] *It is normal that a translation would go through a period during which it would be examined, re-examined, and revised to ensure absolute accuracy. The KJV translators clearly expected the same to be true of their work as well. Yet they held no disdain for the process but rather welcomed it.*

At the same time, they could not understand why others were seeking to alter their translation simply for the sake of argument or disagreement.

If I may be so forward as to point out something else here. The translators obviously did not consider their work to be inspired, preserved, or even the final product. But they certainly did not believe that changes ought to be made simply for the sake of being different.

A number of KJV "revisions" are in print today where it appears as if the supreme motive for changing the text is simply to be different enough to qualify for a new copyright. And once a "new" work has been copyrighted, it can be sold. The love of money truly is the root of all evil!

[66] *Time and again the KJV translators spoke of the need to put a translation through a purging process. In effect, they are admitting that they do not believe their work will be perfect. They believed that they were going to make a good work even better. But in their minds, it was perfectly acceptable to take what they did and improve upon it. Having said that, their idea of "making it better" had to do with bringing a translation more in line with the original Greek and Hebrew.*

way an hindrance to it[67]. This to the cause: then to the persons we say, that of all men they ought to be most silent in this case. For what varieties have they, and what alterations have they made, not only of their Service books, Portesses and Breviaries, but also of their Latin translation? The Service book supposed to be made by S. Ambrose (*Officium Ambrosianum*) was a great while in special use and request; but Pope Hadrian calling a Council with the aid of Charles the Emperor, abolished it, yea, burnt it, and commanded the Service book of Saint Gregory universally to be used [Durand. lib. 5. cap. 2.]. Well, *Officium Gregorianum* gets by this means to be in credit, but doth it continue without change or altering? No, the very *Roman* Service was of two fashions, the New fashion, and the Old, (the one used in one Church, the other in another) as is to be seen in Pamelius a Romanist, his Preface, before *Micrologus*. the same Pamelius reporteth out Radulphus de Rivo, that about the year of our Lord, 1277, Pope Nicolas the Third removed out of the Churches of Rome, the more ancient books (of Service) and brought into use the Missals of the Friers Minorites, and commanded them to be observed there; insomuch that about an hundred years after, when the above name Radulphus happened to be at Rome, he found all the books to be new, (of the new stamp). Neither were there this chopping and changing in the more ancient times only, but also of late: Pius Quintus himself confesseth, that every Bishopric almost had a peculiar kind

---

[67] *What great wisdom! It is refreshing that men of such high education did not allow pride to factor into their thinking. In essence, they were saying that their knowledge and education, even their work in translation was subject to the truth and if necessary, must be corrected by it.*

of service, most unlike to that which others had: which moved him to abolish all other Breviaries, though never so ancient, and privileged and published by Bishops in their Dioceses, and to establish and ratify that only which was of his own setting forth, in the year 1568. Now when the father of their Church, who gladly would heal the sore of the daughter of his people softly and slightly, and make the best of it, findeth so great fault with them for their odds and jarring; we hope the children have no great cause to vaunt of their uniformity. But the difference that appeareth between our translations, and our often correcting of them, is the thing that we are specially charged with; let us see therefore whether they themselves be without fault this way[68], (if it be to be counted a fault, to correct) and whether they be fit men to throw stones at us: *O tandem maior parcas insane minori*: they that are less sound themselves, ought not to object infirmities to others [Horat.]. If we should tell them that Valla, Stapulensis, Erasmus, and Vives found fault with their vulgar translation, and consequently wished the same to be mended, or a new one to be made, they would answer peradventure, that we produced their enemies for witnesses against them;

---

[68] *Interesting argument. It is an argument that I think would be worthy of use even today.*

To those who do not believe that the KJV is a faithful translation, we should ask, "Then, do you have a faithful translation to replace it with?"

Their answer, if they would be consistent, would have to be "No." For they do not believe that they even have a pure Greek text from which to translate. So how could they believe they have a good translation?

*Additionally, for the most part, they do not believe they will **ever** have a perfect text for they are still trying to recover what God says can never be lost!*

albeit, they were in no other sort enemies, than as S. Paul was to the Galatians, for telling them the truth [Gal 4:16]: and it were to be wished, that they had dared to tell it them plainlier and oftener. But what will they say to this, that Pope Leo the Tenth allowed Erasmus' translation of the New Testament, so much different from the vulgar, by his Apostolic Letter and Bull; that the same Leo exhorted Pagnine to translate the whole Bible, and bare whatsoever charges was necessary for the work [Sixtus Senens.] ? Surely, as the Apostle reasoneth to the Hebrews, that if the former Law and Testament had been sufficient, there had been no need of the latter: [Heb 7:11 and 8:7] so we may say, that if the old vulgar had been at all points allowable, to small purpose had labor and charges been undergone, about framing of a new. If they say, it was one Pope's private opinion, and that he consulted only himself; then we are able to go further with them, and to aver, that more of their chief men of all sorts, even their own Trent champions Paiva and Vega, and their own Inquisitors, Hieronymus ab Oleastro, and their own Bishop Isidorus Clarius, and their own Cardinal Thomas a Vio Caietan, do either make new translations themselves, or follow new ones of other men's making, or note the vulgar Interpreter for halting; none of them fear to dissent from him, nor yet to except against him. And call they this an uniform tenor of text and judgment about the text, so many of their Worthies disclaiming the now received conceit? Nay, we will yet come nearer the quick: doth not their Paris edition differ from the Lovaine, and Hentenius his from them both, and yet all of them allowed by authority? Nay, doth not Sixtus Quintus confess, that certain Catholics (he meaneth certain of his own side) were in such an humor of translating the Scriptures into Latin, that Satan taking occasion by them, though they thought of no such matter, did strive what he could, out of so uncertain and manifold a variety of translations, so to mingle all things, that nothing might seem to be left certain and firm in them, etc. [Sixtus 5. praefat. fixa Bibliis.]? Nay, further, did not the same Sixtus ordain by an inviolable decree, and that with the counsel and consent of his Cardinals, that the Latin edition of the old and new Testament, which the Council of Trent would have to be authentic, is the same without controversy which he then set forth, being diligently corrected and printed in the Printing-house of Vatican? Thus Sixtus in his Preface before his Bible. And yet Clement the Eighth his immediate successor, publisheth another edition of the Bible, containing in it infinite differences from that of Sixtus, (and many of them weighty and material) and yet this must be authentic by all means. What is to have the faith of our glorious Lord Jesus Christ with Yea or Nay, if this be not? Again, what is sweet harmony and consent, if this be? Therefore, as Demaratus of Corinth advised a great King, before he talked of the dissensions among the Grecians, to compose his domestic broils (for at that time his Queen and his son and heir were at deadly feud with him) so all the while that our adversaries do make so many and so various editions themselves, and do jar so much about the worth and authority of them, they can with no show of equity challenge us for changing and correcting[69].

The Purpose of the Translators, with their Number, Furniture, Care, etc.

But it is high time to leave them, and to show in brief what we proposed to ourselves, and what course we held in this our perusal and survey of the Bible. Truly (good Christian Reader) we never thought from the beginning, that we should need to make a new translation, nor yet to make of a bad one a good one, (for then the imputation of Sixtus had been true in some sort, that our people had been fed with gall of Dragons instead of wine, with whey instead of milk:) but to make a good one better[70], or out of many good ones[71], one princi-

---

[69] *This is very applicable for translators on the field. In one missionary's field of service, there exists at least 18 different translations, none of which are as accurate as they should be. And yet, when the missionary sought to do a better job, he was condemned for sowing discord among the brethren. But how could he be condemned for doing the same thing that 17 other translation teams before him had done?*

[70] *It has been noted that the majority of the KJV is very much the same as Tyndale's translation. It stands to reason that if they were trying to make a good one better, then the Tyndale translation (or possibly the Geneva translation) is what they had in mind to make better.*

[71] *Apparently, the KJV translators had no qualms about looking at various earlier translations as they accomplished their own because they openly stated that their goal was to make one principle good translation from many others.*

pal[72] good one, not justly to be excepted against; that hath been our endeavor, that our mark. To that purpose there were many chosen, that were greater in other men's eyes than in their own, and that sought the truth rather than their own praise. Again, they came or were thought to come to the work, not *exercendi causa* (as one saith) but *exercitati*, that is, learned, not to learn: For the chief overseer and εργοδιωκτης under his Majesty, to whom not only we, but also our whole Church was much bound, knew by his wisdom, which thing also Nazianzen taught so long ago, that it is a preposterous order to teach first and to learn after, yea that to learn and practice together, is neither commendable for the workman, nor safe for the work [Ναζιανζεν εις ρν. επισκ παρουσ., Idem in Apologet.]. Therefore such were thought upon, as could say modestly with Saint Jerome, *Et Hebraeum Sermonem ex parte didicimus, et in Latino pene ab ipsis incunabulis etc. detriti sumus. Both we have learned the Hebrew tongue in part, and in the Latin we have been exercised almost from our very cradle.* S. Jerome maketh no mention of the Greek tongue, wherein yet he did excel, because he translated not the old Testament out of Greek, but out of Hebrew. And in what sort did these assemble? In the trust of their own knowledge, or of their sharpness of wit, or deepness of judgment, as it were in an arm of flesh? At no hand. They trusted in him that hath the key of David, opening and no man

---

[72] *Principle - first in order of importance; main. This was the goal of their new translation. They wanted to produce a translation that was first in order of importance - the main translation. And they succeeded in their task. Who could ever deny the supremacy of the KJV among the plethora of existing translations today?*

shutting; they prayed to the Lord the Father of our Lord, to the effect that S. Augustine did; *O let thy Scriptures be my pure delight, let me not be deceived in them, neither let me deceive by them* [S. Aug. lib. 11. Confess. cap. 2.]. In this confidence, and with this devotion did they assemble together; not too many, lest one should trouble another; and yet many, lest many things haply might escape them. If you ask what they had before them, truly it was the Hebrew text of the Old Testament, the Greek of the New[73]. These are the two golden pipes, or rather conduits, where-through the olive branches empty themselves into the gold[74]. Saint Augustine calleth them precedent, or original tongues [S. August. 3. de doctr. c. 3. etc.]; Saint Jerome, fountains [S. Hieron. ad Suniam et Fretel.]. The same Saint Jerome affirmeth, and Gratian hath not spared to put it into his Decree, That *as the credit of the old Books* (he meaneth of the Old Testament) *is to be tried by the Hebrew Volumes, so of the New by the Greek tongue,* he meaneth by the original Greek [S. Hieron. ad Lucinium, Dist. 9 ut veterum.]. If truth be to be tried by these tongues, then whence should a translation be made, but out of them? These tongues therefore, the Scriptures we say in those tongues, we set before us to translate, being the tongues wherein God was pleased

---

[73] *The Greek and Hebrew were the standard by which every word choice was measured. Though they obviously consulted other translations, it was the Greek and Hebrew to which the work must be measured.*

[74] *Very clearly, the translators believed that the original languages are the vehicle by which God has delivered His truth to man. This may be reflected in a translation, but the source is still the Greek and Hebrew.*

to speak to his Church by his Prophets and Apostles[75]. Neither did we run over the work with that posting haste that the Septuagint did [76], if that be true which is reported of them, that they finished it in 72 days [Joseph. Antiq. lib. 12.]; neither were we barred or hindered from going over it again, having once done it, like S. Jerome, if that be true which himself reporteth, that he could no sooner write anything, but presently it was caught from him, and published, and he could not have leave to mend it [S. Hieron. ad Pammac. pro libr. advers. Iovinian.]: neither, to be short, were we the first that fell in hand with translating the Scripture into English, and consequently destitute of former helps, as it is written of Origen, that he was the first [πρωτοπειροι] in a manner, that put his hand to write Commentaries upon the Scriptures, and therefore no marvel, if he overshot himself many times[77]. None of these things: the work hath not been huddled up in 72 days, but hath cost the workmen, as light as it seemeth, the pains of twice seven times seventy two days and more: matters of such

---

[75] *Contrary to those who are of the opinion that it is acceptable to make a translation from a translation, the KJV Translators apparently believed that the original languages should be the basis.*

[76] *It took more than 3 years to finish the work of translating the King James Version. This is a testament to several things: First, their care in translation. Each verse, each word, checked and double-checked for accuracy; second, that the translators were not moved by double-inspiration, or, advanced revelation, for if they were, they should have completed the work in a far shorter time.*

[77] *Ah, to be the first to accomplish a great feat! For many, this would sound like a great honor. And maybe it is. But in the area of translation, it is also a frightful thing for a translator has nothing compare his work with. It is far better to have other works to consult than to have nothing to consult.*

weight and consequence are to be speeded with maturity: for in a business of moment a man feareth not the blame of convenient slackness [φιλει γαρ οκνειν πραγμ' ανηρ πρασσων ηεγα, Sophoc. in Elect.]. Neither did we think much to consult the Translators or Commentators[78], Chaldee, Hebrew, Syrian, Greek or Latin, no nor the Spanish, French, Italian, or Dutch; neither did we disdain to revise that which we had done[79], and to bring back to the anvil that which we had hammered: but having and using as great helps as were needful, and fearing no reproach for slowness, nor coveting praise for expedition, we have at the length, through the good hand of the Lord upon us, brought the work to that pass that you see.

Reasons Moving Us To Set Diversity of Senses in the Margin, where there is Great Probability for Each

Some peradventure would have no variety of senses to be set in the margin, lest the authority of the Scriptures for deciding of controversies by that show of uncertain-

---

[78] *No doubt they would have disagreed with the opinions of commentators, yet they still used them. It is helpful to have as many opinions on a text as possible when the text is somewhat difficult or vague.*

[79] *They did not consider their work to be "inspired" for if they did, they would not have believed they could go back and revise something they had already accomplished beforehand.*

ty, should somewhat be shaken[80]. But we hold their judgment not to be so sound in this point. For though, *whatsoever things are necessary are manifest,* as S. Chrysostom saith [παντα τα αναγκαια δηλα, S. Chrysost. in 2 Thess. cap. 2.], and as S. Augustine, *In those things that are plainly set down in the Scriptures, all such matters are found that concern Faith, Hope, and Charity* [S. Aug. 2. de doctr. Christ. cap. 9.]. Yet for all that it cannot be dissembled, that partly to exercise and whet our wits, partly to wean the curious from loathing of them for their every-where plainness, partly also to stir up our devotion to crave the assistance of God's spirit by prayer, and lastly, that we might be forward to seek aid of our brethren by conference, and never scorn those that be not in all respects so complete as they should be, being to seek in many things ourselves, it hath pleased God in his divine providence, here and there to scatter words and sentences of that difficulty and doubtfulness, not in doctrinal points that concern salvation, (for in such it hath been vouched that the Scriptures are plain) but in matters of less moment, that fearfulness would better beseem us than confidence[81], and if we will resolve, to resolve upon modesty with S. Augustine, (though not in this same

---

[80] *Even the KJV translators would have balked at the idea that their choices were the **only** possibilities. This is why they had margin notes. In doing so, they were aware that some would even wish that margin notes were not given for fear that their very existence would undermine the authority of the translation.*

Yet humility and piety would not allow them to hide the truth. In this respect, they wanted to leave it up to the reader, with guidance of God's Spirit, to determine which reading is the correct reading.

[81] *So, it was humility that led the translators to use margin notes.*

case altogether, yet upon the same ground) *Melius est dubitare de occultis, quam litigare de incertis* [S. Aug li. 8. de Genes. ad liter. cap. 5.], *it is better to make doubt of those things which are secret, than to strive about those things that are uncertain.* There be many words in the Scriptures, which be never found there but once, (having neither brother nor neighbor [ipax legomena], as the Hebrews speak) so that we cannot be holpen by conference of places. Again, there be many rare names of certain birds, beasts and precious stones, etc. concerning which the Hebrews themselves are so divided among themselves for judgment, that they may seem to have defined this or that, rather because they would say something, than because they were sure of that which they said[82], as S. Jerome somewhere saith of the Septuagint. Now in such a case, doth not a margin do well to admonish the Reader to seek further, and not to conclude or dogmatize upon this or that peremptorily? For as it is a fault of incredulity, to doubt of those things that are evident: so to determine of such things as the Spirit of God hath left (even in the judgment of the judicious) questionable, can be no less than presumption. Therefore as S. Augustine saith, that variety of translations is profitable for the finding out of the sense of the

---

[82] *In other words, when it came to commentators, in many cases, it came down to making a logical guess. Knowing this, they feared that they would make the wrong one. Thus, they left it in the hands of the student of the Scriptures to come to their own decision.*

Scriptures [S. Aug. 2. De doctr. Christian. cap. 14.][83]: so diversity of signification and sense in the margin, where the text is no so clear, must needs do good, yea, is necessary, as we are persuaded[84]. We know that Sixtus Quintus expressly forbiddeth, that any variety of readings of their vulgar edition, should be put in the margin [Sixtus 5. praef. Bibliae.], (which though it be not altogether the same thing to that we have in hand, yet it looketh that way) but we think he hath not all of his own side his favorers, for this conceit. They that are wise, had rather have their judgments at liberty in differences of readings, than to be captivated to one, when it may be the other. If they were sure that their high Priest had all laws shut up in his breast, as Paul the Second bragged [Plat. in Paulo secundo.], and that he were as free from error by special privilege, as the Dictators of Rome were made by law inviolable, it were another matter; then his word were an Oracle, his opinion a decision. But the eyes of the world are now open, God be thanked, and have been a great while [ομοιοπαθης τρωτος γ οι χρως εστι.], they find that he is subject to the same affections and infirmities that others be, that his skin is penetrable, and therefore so

---

[83] *There are those who disdain the further study of words or phrases claiming that the English meaning is all that the Greek or Hebrew could possibly mean in a particular setting. Apparently, the KJV translators did not believe this and thought that the reader should know when deeper study might be warranted.*

[84] *The translators did not claim perfection in their translation. In fact, they clearly understood that further clarification may be needed. In other words, they did not see their work as the finished product, although in essence, it was.*

much as he proveth, not as much as he claimeth, they grant and embrace[85].

Reasons Inducing Us Not To Stand Curiously upon an Identity of Phrasing

Another thing we think good to admonish thee of (gentle Reader) that we have not tied ourselves to an uniformity of phrasing, or to an identity of words, as some peradventure would wish that we had done, because they observe, that some learned men somewhere, have been as exact as they could that way. Truly, that we might not vary from the sense of that which we had translated before, if the word signified the same thing in both places (for there be some words that be not of the same sense everywhere [πολυσημα]) we were especially careful, and made a conscience, according to our duty. But, that we should express the same notion in the same particular word; as for example, if we translate the Hebrew or Greek word once by *Purpose*, never to call it *Intent*; if one where *Journeying*, never *Traveling*; if one where *Think*, never *Suppose*; if one where *Pain*, never *Ache*; if one where *Joy*, never *Gladness*, etc[86]. Thus to mince the matter, we thought to savour more of curiosity than wisdom, and that rather it would breed scorn in the Atheist, than bring profit to the godly

---

[85] *A clear rejection of Papal authority.*

[86] *I have heard the charge made that the KJV Translators were not consistent in that they would often employ several translations for one word. For example: "pisteuo" is usually translated as "believe" but in several places, they chose "trust". But the translators allowed for this type of variation insofar as the translation itself remained accurate. Variety cannot be used as an argument against consistency or accuracy.*

Reader. For is the kingdom of God become words or syllables? why should we be in bondage to them if we may be free, use one precisely when we may use another no less fit, as commodiously[87]? A godly Father in the Primitive time showed himself greatly moved, that one of newfangledness called κραββατον, "σκιμπους" ["a bed"; Niceph. Calist. lib.8. cap.42.], though the difference be little or none; and another reporteth that he was much abused for turning *Cucurbita* (to which reading the people had been used) into *Hedera* [S. Hieron. in 4. Ionae. See S. Aug. epist. 10.]. Now if this happen in better times, and upon so small occasions, we might justly fear hard censure, if generally we should make verbal and unnecessary changings. We might also be charged (by scoffers) with some unequal dealing towards a great number of good English words. For as it is written of a certain great Philosopher, that he should say, that those logs were happy that were made images to be worshipped; for their fellows, as good as they, lay for blocks behind the fire: so if we should say, as it were, unto certain words, Stand up higher, have a place in the Bible always, and to others of like quality, Get ye hence, be banished forever, we might be taxed peradventure with S. James his words, namely, *To be partial in ourselves and judges of evil thoughts.* Add hereunto, that niceness in words was always counted the next step to trifling, and so was to be curious about names too: also that we cannot follow a better pattern for elocution than God himself; therefore he using divers words, in his holy writ, and indifferently

---

[87] *In other words, they did not use the same word in every case purely for variety and readability. Yet they did not sacrifice accuracy for readability sake either.*

for one thing in nature [leptologia;/ adolescia;/ το σρουδαξεινεπι ονομασι; see Euseb. προπαρασκευ. li. 12. ex Platon.]: we, if we will not be superstitious, may use the same liberty in our English versions out of Hebrew and Greek, for that copy or store that he hath given us. Lastly, we have on the one side avoided the scrupulosity of the Puritans, who leave the old Ecclesiastical words, and betake them to other, as when they put *Washing* for *Baptism*[88], and *Congregation* instead of *Church*: as also on the other side we have shunned the obscurity of the Papists, in their *Azimes, Tunike, Rational, Holocausts, Praepuce, Pasche*, and a number of such like, whereof their late translation is full, and that of purpose to darken the sense, that since they must needs translate the Bible, yet by the language thereof, it may be kept from being understood. But we desire that the Scripture may speak like itself, as in the language of Canaan, that it may be understood even of the very vulgar[89].

Many other things we might give thee warning of (gentle Reader) if we had not exceeded the measure of a Preface already. It remaineth, that we commend thee to God, and to the Spirit of his grace, which is able to build further than we can ask or think. He removeth the

---

[88] *The translators saw no need to translate the word "baptizo" into "wash" or "immerse" since it was an established ecclesiastic term. The same could be said of the word "eklesia" which they did not change to "assembly" or "congregation", but chose to keep the established term "church". If it wasn't wrong, they didn't change it.*

[89] *It is not that the translation was placed in an easy-to-read format but that it was now possible for the "very vulgar" (lowest educated, common man) should be able to have an understanding of God's message since it would now be in the English language.*

scales from our eyes, the veil from our hearts, opening our wits that we may understand his word, enlarging our hearts, yea correcting our affections, that we may love it above gold and silver, yea that we may love it to the end. Ye are brought unto fountains of living water which ye digged not; do not cast earth into them with the Philistines, neither prefer broken pits before them with the wicked Jews. [Gen 26:15. Jer 2:13.] Others have laboured, and you may enter into their labours; O receive not so great things in vain, O despise not so great salvation! Be not like swine to tread under foot so precious things, neither yet like dogs to tear and abuse holy things. Say not to our Saviour with the Gergesites, Depart out of our coasts [Matt 8:34]; neither yet with Esau sell your birthright for a mess of pottage [Heb 12:16]. If light be come into the world, love not darkness more than light; if food, if clothing be offered, go not naked, starve not yourselves. Remember the advice of Nazianzene, *It is a grievous thing* (or dangerous) *to neglect a great fair, and to seek to make markets afterwards* [Ναζιανζ. περι αγ. βαπτ. δεινον πανηγυριν παρελθειν και τηνικαυτα πραγματειαν επιζητειν]: also the encouragement of S. Chrysostom, *It is altogether impossible, that he that is sober* (and watchful) *should at any time be neglected* [S. Chrysost. in epist. ad Rom. cap. 14. orat. 26. in ηθικ. αμηχανον σφοδρα αμηχανον]: Lastly, the admonition and menacing of S. Augustine, *They that despise God's will inviting them, shall feel God's will taking vengeance of them.* It is a fearful thing to fall into the hands of the living God; [Heb 10:31] but a blessed thing it is, and will bring us to everlasting blessedness in the end, when God speaketh unto us, to hearken; when he setteth his word before us, to read it; when he stretcheth out his hand and calleth, to answer, Here am I, here we are to do thy will, O God. The Lord work a care and conscience in us to know him and serve him, that we may be acknowledged of him at the appearing of our Lord Jesus Christ, to whom with the holy Ghost, be all praise and thanksgiving. Amen.[90]

---

[90] *Much has been said about the "archaic" Elizabethan English style of the KJV. It is said that the prose of the KJV reflects the English style of long ago and should be updated to reflect the modern way of speaking English. Yet this very preface was written at the same time the translation was written and the style is substantially different. It stands to reason that the translators purposefully wrote in a more respectful and poetic style (most likely out of respect for the King's speech). After all, it is the Word of God and it deserves our very best!*

Commentator's Epilogue

Admittedly, some of my commentary/footnotes are repetitive but the points bear repeating. No doubt, my opinions will cause some to rejoice and others to reject.

But I think I have clarity in this area having been working in the field of translation for some time now.

The Bible says that Jesus sets us free. And in the matters of faith and practice, this is true.

But if I may take the liberty to express myself in a similar way. Knowledge sets a translator free. If the processes and philosophies expressed here in this short book would be considered, it is my belief that a modern translator will find a certain level of freedom from the limitation often placed on us by others.

If we want to produce a translation in any language that is as good as the KJV in English, then we will need to approach the work of translation in the same way. I strongly recommend that a close examination of this letter be made before any translator, or translation team begins their work.

CPSIA information can be obtained
at www.ICGtesting.com
Printed in the USA
LVHW091558291220
675341LV00004B/1121